I'M NOT DEFECTIVE
THE STORY OF JOSH

NEAL WOOTEN

ISBN 978-1-61225-291-9

©Copyright 2015 Tina Lythgoe/Neal Wooten
All rights reserved

Cover image of Josh designed by Nicolas Peruzzo.

Bibliography:
"Meet Adorable Josh: Runner up in our Cover Dog Contest!" Modern Dog Magazine. Winter 2014

Dr. Patrick Mahaney. "Cleft Palate in Dogs Awareness." www.petmd.com

No part of this publication may be reproduced in any form or stored, transmitted or recorded by any means without the written permission of the author.

Published by Mirror Publishing
Milwaukee, WI 53214

Printed in the USA.

I'm Josh's mom, Tina, and I want to thank several people for their support.

My mom and dad, John & Rita Lythgoe, for showing me so much love as a child and allowing me to have so many animals. I'm blessed to be able to give that love back today to everything that comes my way.

Sandy at Tunica Humane Society. When I started Josh's FB page, you were the first to help. I will never forget it.

My best friend and niece, Skyler Barberio, for always being there for me when I'm sad and happy.

Candice Lowry. You have always been there for me and helped me over the years no matter what.

My love, Lenny Leichtweisz, for never saying no to me, for always picking up animals from the shelters, and for not getting upset when I have to wake us up every two hours to feed motherless critters.

Toby Wisneski from Leave No Paws Behind (LNPB) for pulling Josh to safety, taking a chance on him, and for placing him in my hands.

My fellow humanitarians, Glenys Drayton and Sandy Kidman from Conni Critters/Conni USA, for helping all creatures great and small.

My wonderful friends: Glenda Mosner, LeeAnna Longwolf, Margaret Cummings, Donna Mary Nicholls, Karen Doonan, Carole Flynn, Mike Graham, Munster, and Brogan: My Life as a Therapy Dog for always being there for me.

Josh for being such a fighter and not giving up. You are the light of my life.

And of course the great and brilliant Neal Wooten for writing this book and helping me spread the word of hope and inspiration. You are a saint.

Other books by author Neal Wooten

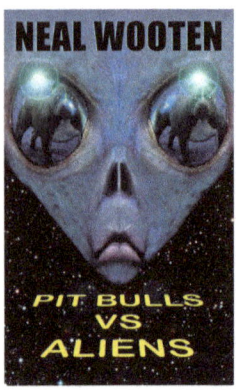

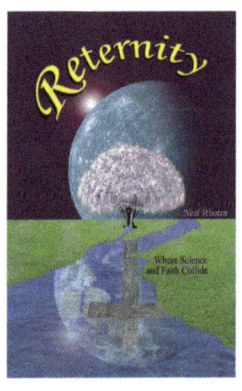
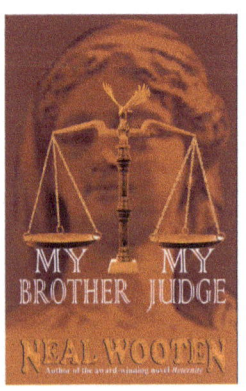

Find Josh and his family on Facebook at:
https://www.facebook.com/pages/
Josh-and-his-critters/1506300642923754

Room for One More Dog

I see by his coat he must be a stray
The untidy look gives him away
He's lost his will and is so thin
Hasn't eaten since God knows when
I know as I coax him through the door
There's always room for just one more

The other night in the freezing rain
That little female came again
Matted and soaked, crying in need
Lost and alone with babies to feed
Her pleading eyes, I couldn't ignore
There's always room for just one more

There's the poor doggy, standing in the rain
I've tried to entice him time and again
One ears lopsided, the other's been torn
Blind in one eye, lost and forlorn
He's coming now, so I'll open the door
There's always room for just one more

These stories are true as I've said before
There's always room for just one more.

Author Unknown

CHAPTER 1
A Pup Named Josh

"He's on death row."

Tina's heart sank. It was mid-afternoon on the 20th of January, 2014, when the call came in from Toby Wisneski, the CEO of a rescue group called *Leave No Paws Behind* (LNPB).

"I have to tell you," Toby continued, "he's a cleft-palate puppy. He's only a few hours old and if I can't find someone to take him tonight, they will kill him. The breeder just dropped him off after he was born to be put to sleep."

Of course, Tina thought. *He's not worth any money and who needs a high vet bill?* "Yes," she blurted out without thinking or even knowing exactly what a "cleft-palate puppy" was. She didn't have to think. It was a dog in need.

Tina worked at her mom's grooming business, Rita's Grooming, where she had been for the last twenty-eight years. She was known throughout the community as "Momma Tina" because she will rescue anything—literally. She's even rescued a few humans and has the Humanitarian Award to prove it. Thank goodness her job allows her to take her critters back and forth to work with her.

Having donated lots of time working with LNPB as a foster mom or providing Hospice care, as well as providing free grooming to all the dogs they rescue, Tina knew they had no facility, which means the only way they can pull a dog from the pound is to have a foster parent readily available. With euthanasia looming, she quickly stepped up to the plate. Of course she needed a pinch hitter.

"Let me talk to Lenny," Tina said.

Toby put Lenny on. Lenny is a transport driver for LNPB—and Tina's husband.

"Are you going after this boy for me?" Tina asked. Tina is a striking woman whom some say resembles a young Elvira. Her dark eyes and big beautiful smile are complimented by her long black hair. Via the telephone, however, she relied on her sultry voice.

Lenny is a big fella with a real man's mustache who would look right at home on a big Harley Davidson sporting a leather jacket, but he knew he didn't stand a chance here. "Yes, I'm leaving now." It was a cold winter day, especially for California, as he hopped in his car and drove an hour and a half to Camarillo in

Ventura County to pick up the little guy.

"I'm here to pick up the puppy with the palate problem," he said as he entered the pound. The shelter is a nice facility with fenced areas for the dogs to get exercise and with a loyal and dedicated staff. But like many shelters in California, they don't have the resources to care for every dog that came their way.

"Sure thing," the guy said and walked away. He came back carrying a shoebox and handed it over. "There you go."

Lenny opened the box and looked inside. "Uh… I'm here to pick up a dog, not a kitten."

The guy laughed. "That is a dog."

Lenny looked inside again at the tiny ball of fur the size of his thumb. "Okay, if you say so." He signed the paperwork and walked back to his vehicle with the shoebox in hand. As he pulled out of the parking lot, he called Tina.

"Do you have him?" Tina was on pins and needles.

"Well, I guess I do," Lenny said.

"What do you mean?"

Lenny glanced down at the shoebox and shook his head. "I still say it's a cat."

He drove back to Los Angeles and took the shoebox with the dog, or cat, or whatever it was straight to the veterinarian. Easy Valley Veterinary Clinic is right next door to Rita's Grooming.

"There's really nothing we can do at this point," Dr. Hohne said. He opened the dog's mouth and pointed his little flashlight inside. "He has a crack on the right side of the roof of his mouth. All you can do is try to feed him."

Lenny took the box with the small ball of fur home to Tina.

"Oh my god," Tina gasped. "He's so tiny." She looked up and Lenny with a lump in her throat. "How am I going to keep this little guy alive?"

Mommy-mode kicked in and luckily she had some powdered milk on hand. She knew goat's milk was also good and could be picked up at your local grocery store, but to never give them cow's milk Their little tummies can't take it.

"Are you going to tube feed him?" Lenny asked.

Tube feeding is where you put a small tube down the throat all the way to the belly and literally push the milk right to where it's needed.

"I don't know," Tina said. "Let's try a bottle first." She took a very small bottle that she kept on hand for tiny critters and put it to the puppy's mouth.

One small drop at a time, the puppy was taking it.

"Whew." Tina breathed a sigh of relief. After he had enough, she took warm cotton balls and caressed his genitals to simulate the actions of a momma dog to make the puppy go potty. This must be done every time after feeding at this stage.

"I just hope he makes it through the night," Tina said mostly to herself.

She placed him in a warm little bed and ten minutes later he began to cry.

Is he in pain? Tina wondered. She picked him up and he stopped. She put him back to bed and fifteen minutes later he began to cry again. This time she let him cry thinking it would eventually subside. It didn't. In fact, it got louder. She picked him up and once again he stopped crying. It was obvious he wanted someone to hold him. Tina lay in her bed watching TV with the puppy on her chest until he went to sleep.

She knew puppies this age needed to be fed every two hours so she decided to stay up all night. That was it. That was all it took. They bonded.

"Well, little fellow, you made it through the night." Tina smiled seeing the light of morning floating through the curtains.

For the next five days, Tiny spent as many hours as she could with the puppy. Finally confident that he was going to live, she sent an email to Toby at LNPB.

It was a short email with one message in Spanish. When the CEO emailed back to ask what the Spanish phrase meant, Tina replied, "Foster Fail."

"Oh, no," she messaged back. "What does that mean?"

Tina smiled and typed: "It means I can't provide just a foster home for him. I'm in love. I'm keeping him." She reached down and gently caressed the puppy. She had a hundred name ideas in mind but decided to stick with the name the pound had already given him. "You're home, Josh. You're home."

CHAPTER 2
Lucky Charm

"We can call off the trip," Lenny said. "I know you're worried about Josh. Your mom will understand."

Tina caressed the little fur ball in her lap, who purred as he dozed comfortably. It had only been seven days since she had decided to keep him. She looked up at her husband and smiled. "No, we've been planning this trip for a long time. Besides, he's coming with us."

Lenny knew not to argue.

The next day, Tina, her mom Rita, her husband Lenny, Josh, a baby pigeon, a baby squirrel, and a fifteen-year-old Poodle/Jack Russell mix named Lambchop, piled into the car and drove to San Diego. Like Josh, Lambchop was a rescue from death row via Leave No Paws Behind.

Once they arrived, they checked into their room at the casino hotel Harrah's Rincon, the only pet-friendly casino there. This is something Tina's mom had taught her and the only place they stay.

"Hurry, I need to feed Josh." Tina was getting anxious as she watched Lenny fumble with the keycard.

"I hate these things," Lenny said as he slid the card again. This time the green light came on and he pushed open the door and grabbed their bags.

Tina walked in and went straight to the bed. She took Josh out of his little carrier and placed him on the bedspread. As she started preparing his milk, she noticed something.

"Lenny!" she yelled.

Lenny dropped the bags. "What? What's wrong?"

Tina was jumping up and down. "His eye is open. His eye is open."

Lenny leaned down to look. "Well, I'll be. It is."

Just the corner of the left eye was open barely enough for his curious eyeball to scan the panoramic view of his immediate surroundings.

"Isn't that awesome, Lenny?" Tina asked.

"Yeah, great. Let's go to the casino."

Tina made sure everyone was comfy and they left the room for the lights and thrills of the casino. They each went their different ways. Tina walked around a while before settling in front of a slot machine. Before she could put her coins in, however, her phone rang. It was her mother.

"Come quick!" Rita shouted. "I just won five thousand dollars on Keno."

Tina almost fell off her chair. She called Lenny and they both met her at the Keno board.

"Here," Rita said as she handed Tina and Lenny one thousand dollars each.

"Oh my gosh," Tina said and began to cry.

The day had begun great. Tina played poker for a while until it was time to go back and feed Josh and the others. Having saved Josh from death row and her mom winning big, she knew her luck had reached its limits. But she was satisfied.

As she passed a weird machine named *4 Double 4*, something made her stop. "No, I have to go feed," she said to the machine. "I don't want to play you." But she kept walking closer. It was like an out-of-body experience. She could see herself getting closer and hear herself saying "No." Maybe it was having four animals in her room that drew her to the strange machine.

She put in twenty dollars. Nothing. Again. Nothing. On the third tap, the machine froze.

"What the heck?" Tina looked over the machine to find out what happened. There were no bells, no lights, nothing. Then she saw the wording on the machine: "Call Attendant."

An attendant, a pretty woman all in black, arrived. "Congratulations."

"What?" Tina asked. "Did I win?"

The attendant nodded. "Yes, you just won eight thousand dollars."

Tina burst into tears again. "Are you sure?"

The lady laughed. "Yes, I'm sure."

Tina thought of Josh. "How long will it take because I have a baby to feed?"

"Hold out your hand," the attendant said and counted out the money on the spot.

Tina rushed to the room, calling Lenny and Rita from the elevator. "Meet me in the room," was all she could manage.

Lenny and Rita walked into the room as Tina was feeding Josh. Tina raised him up in front of her. "Say hello to my lucky charm. I just won eight thousand dollars." She kissed Josh on the head. "Maybe I should change your name to Jackpot."

Tina gave Rita and Lenny a thousand dollars each. As they went back to the casino, Tina stopped at the machine and looked at it as if to say "thank you." Then she shrugged. "What the heck?" she whispered. She put in another twenty and hit another thousand dollars. She almost passed out.

I'm Not Defective: The Story of Josh

As the attendant was paying her this time, the VIP Host walked up, a sharply dressed business man.

"Hello. I'm Jamison Blake. Congratulations on your success."

Tina blushed. "Thank you. I think I owe it to my lucky charm, a little puppy I just rescued."

"Really?" Mr. Blake's eyes lit up. "I rescue dogs myself. And cats and goats too."

Wow. Tina had found a kindred spirit. She took Mr. Blake to her room and introduced him to Josh and told him the story. Needless to say he was overwhelmed. He took out his cellphone and dialed.

"Yes, this is Jamison Blake. Please get the penthouse ready. Mrs. Lythgoe and her entire crew will be checking in in five minutes." He smiled at Tina, who was crying yet again. "You won't ever stay in this room again. Here's my cell number. Call anytime." He kissed Josh on the head and said, "You just went from the pound to the penthouse."

The bell desk sent staff members up to move all their stuff for them. There were no numbers in the elevator for their new quarters, just the letters "PH." They had the entire floor. As the bellhops pushed open the two huge doors, Rita began to cry along with Tina. It was like paradise; huge chandeliers and three huge bathrooms, each with a Jacuzzi.

"Holy crap," was all Lenny could muster.

They had the time of their lives. "You truly are my lucky charm," Tina said to Josh as they got into the car to go home.

On the way home, she received a text from Mr. Blake. "Please let me know when you're coming back. And please bring Josh each time."

There was little doubt that Mr. Blake had fallen in love with Josh. Tina knew the feeling all too well.

It was a day they would not ever forget. Tina and Rita even managed to leave with most of their winnings. As for Lenny, well he made out okay too. He came home with two thousand dollars; the amounts that Tina and Rita had given him, which he wisely kept in his pocket and spent the day at the casino swimming pool.

CHAPTER 3
World Meet Josh

"What do you think; a westie mix?"

Tina watched Josh run around with another small dog at her mom's grooming business. They were having a ball chasing each other. Josh, now two months old, had many dog friends that came to visit him. In fact, people without pets would even stop by often just to check to see if Josh was there so they could spend time with him. He loved the attention and had no idea that he was any different at all. Of course he was different, even his bark, which was more of a high-pitched whine.

Tina looked up and smiled at her mom. "Yeah, I was thinking that too. Maybe a West Highland Terrier mix."

"Well, he's sure unique," her mom said.

Tina nodded. "That's putting it mildly. His left eye is cocked and wanders, his front feet are huge, his back feet are teeny-tiny, his tail is abnormally long, he has extra teeth on one side and missing teeth on the other, and his breath is worse than any dog I've ever known, probably because of the crack in the top of his mouth."

"So?" her mom asked. "What are you saying?"

Tina laughed. "I'm saying he's the most beautiful thing I've ever seen."

After work that day, Tina went home with Josh and Lambchop. These two always accompanied her to work. Josh couldn't wait to get home to play with his three sisters, all older poodle mixes that were also foster fails.

"Take it easy on them," Tina said as Josh bolted for the trio.

Josh was so full of energy that it sometimes was a little rough for the older dogs to keep up with him. Oddly enough, in the beginning, Tina had to keep Josh hidden from them because they didn't accept him. Apparently, like Lenny, they all thought he was a kitten too.

"Come on, Josh, let's give your sisters a rest and go to the park."

Josh knew what that meant and he jumped up and down as Tina put on the leash. As they entered the park, which is right across the street from their house, Tina took off the leash. Zoom! Josh loves the park. He runs so fast that it appears as if his feet don't touch the ground. He becomes a different dog—one with no limitations at all.

That evening, as Tina was checking her emails and Facebook, she realized that Josh was getting more messages than she was. "Look at this," she said to Lenny. "'How's Josh? Post more pictures of Josh. I love Josh.' It goes on and on."

Lenny laughed. "He's popular. Maybe it's time you started a Facebook page for him."

Tina couldn't believe she hadn't thought of it before. She had plenty of photos, so she sat right there at the computer until his fan page was live and then let many of her friends know about it.

Glancing up at the clock, she realized it was past 8 p.m., past her bedtime. She got ready for bed and climbed under the covers. That was Josh's cue. He rushed to the bed and tried to jump up. Lenny and Tina couldn't help but laugh. Try as he might, Josh just wasn't big enough yet, so Tina helped him up.

Of course Josh never went to sleep. He would just play with one of his toys, of which he was very protective, until the wee hours of the night. Every morning Tina always struggled to get him up.

The next day Tina went to work with Josh and Lambchop as usual. She had forgotten about setting up the Facebook account for Josh. It dawned on her just before she got off work that day. Arriving back home, she signed on and was shocked. Josh already had several hundred fans. There were several messages addressed to Josh and several posts asking Josh to like their page as well.

Over the next few weeks, it continued to grow even more. Tina was amazed at the outpouring of love for her little guy, but was even more moved by the fact that Josh seemed to be an inspiration to others. Here was one message Josh received:

> Hey Josh and Josh's Mom! I just felt in my heart to send you a short message. You have touched my heart with your story in more ways than you will ever know! I never talk to anyone online that I don't know but I feel different with you! First of all, I was born with a cleft palate and had three major surgeries as a child. Second of all, I had a best friend who was named Josh who died of a disease called Cystic Fibrosis. So that being said, I want you to know that I am praying for you every day and I am so happy your mom saved you Josh!

I'm Not Defective: The Story of Josh

```
God has plans for you! You and
your mom inspire me!! Love you
sweet Josh!
```

```
Carla Marie Whatley
```

Tina wiped a tear from her eye. She looked down at Josh who was staring up at her. "You sure have an effect on people, don't you?"

Josh's fan base continued to grow. By the time he was three and a half months old, he had over five thousand fans. Tina discovered that there were so many wonderful supportive people all around the world.

One day she decided to enter him into the Cover Dog Contest for *Modern Dog Magazine*, the winner of which would appear on the cover of a future edition. The contest ran for six weeks and Tina bugged and begged everyone she could think of to vote for little Josh. Four weeks later, it was neck-and-neck with Josh and another dog.

"How's the contest going?" her mom asked one day.

"Too close," Tina said. "We have one hundred thousand votes, but so does another dog. His name is Harley. He's the spokes-dog for the National Dog Mill Rescue and they have a lot of followers." She looked over at Josh who was sitting quietly by Lambchop. "We're not giving up though, are we big boy?"

Josh's floppy ears perked up. He was ready for the fight.

Unfortunately it wasn't to be. Although they finished with an awesome one hundred seventy thousand votes, Harley finished with one hundred eighty-five thousand. Harley would be on the cover. But the magazine was so impressed with Josh's second-place finish they included him in the magazine with a picture and article titled *Meet Adorable Josh: Runner up in our Cover Dog Contest.*

Tina was proud.

Josh just wanted to play.

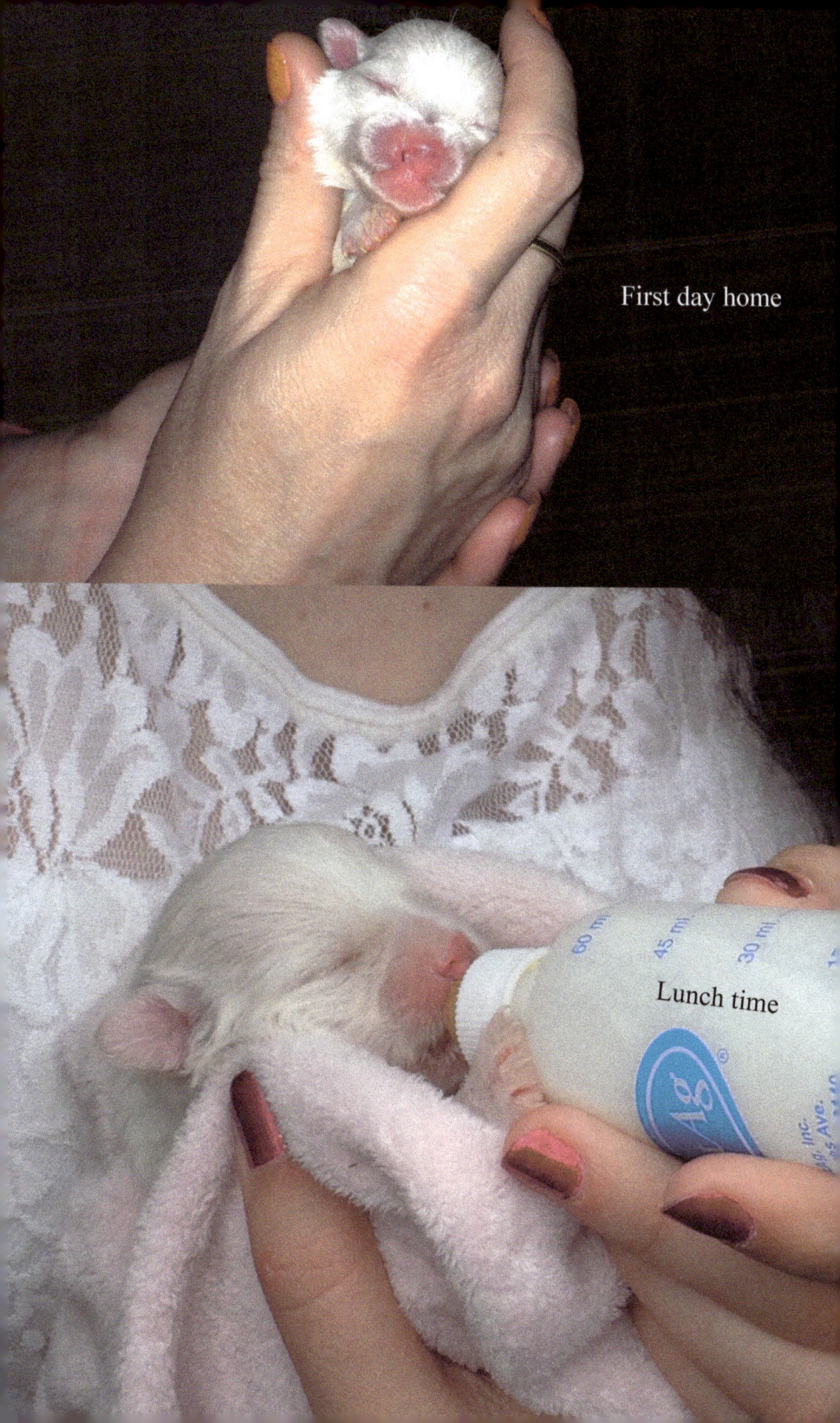

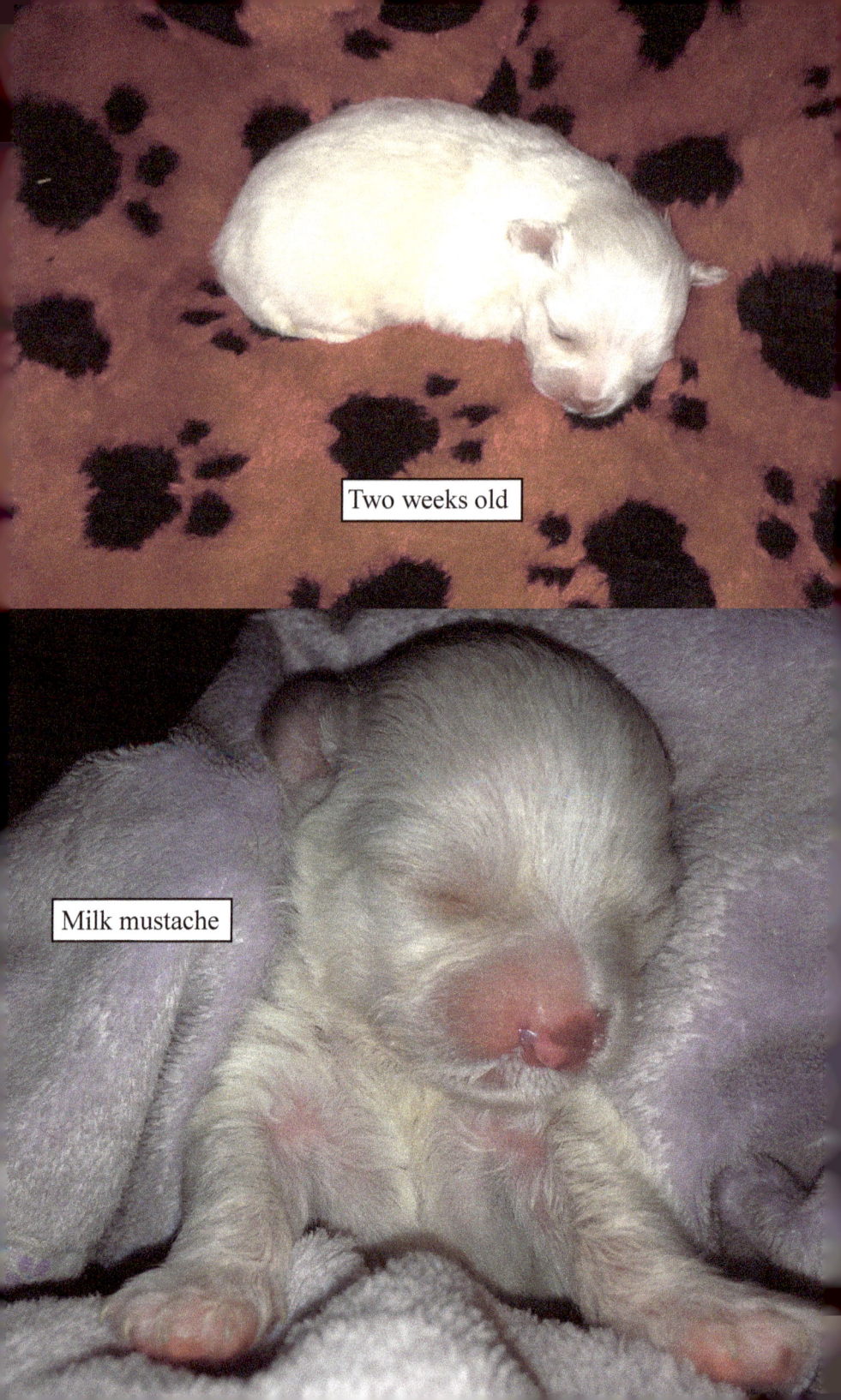

Sixteen days old

At work

With brothers Topogigio the opossum and Fuzzy the cat

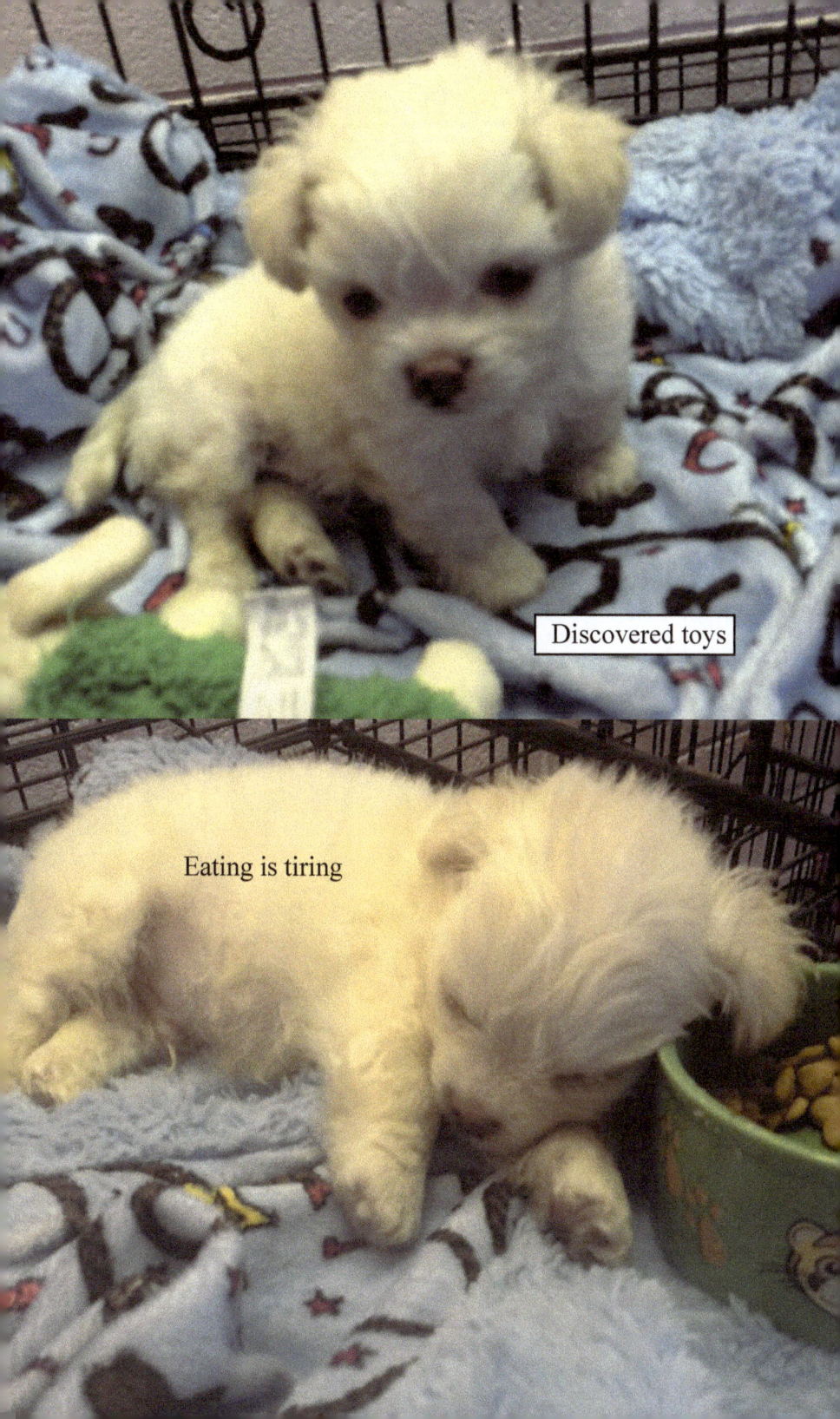

Nap time with Lambchop and Little Pig

Six months old and going to the mall

Groomed and looking good

Smiling for the camera

Story in Modern Dog Magazine

Meet Adorable Josh

Runner up in our Cover Dog Contest!

We felt we'd be remiss not to include a mention of Josh, the runner-up in our Cover Dog Contest with over 170,000 votes. This little dog has won an awful lot of hearts, and with good reason. Josh's momma, Tina Lythgoe, has worked at Rita's Grooming in Sun Valley, CA, for 28 years and takes in all kinds of abandoned critters: baby birds, sparrows, pigeons... whoever needs help. So when Tina got a call about a tiny puppy, just 48 hours old, that needed to be pulled from the pound or face euthanasia, she immediately dispatched her husband, Lenny, to go and pick him up. He took the wee slip of a thing straight to the vet who confirmed the little dog had a cleft palate and that there was nothing to be done but take him home and attempt to feed him. He did great with a bottle, and Tina, for her part, knew the minute she held him that she was keeping him forever. Josh has gone on to become a bit of an internet celebrity, inspiring others to overcome their difficulties, but mostly Tina wants everyone to know that birth defects are surmountable problems. Just look at happy Josh, beloved by not only his family but a ton of others too.

Lenny, so proud of the little man

CHAPTER 4
Look a Gift Dog in the Mouth

"Uh oh," Tina said to her mom. "Josh must have a package today."

Rita looked over and saw Josh staring out the window, his tail wagging uncontrollably. "I guess you're right."

Josh had begun to receive lots of packages delivered to Rita's Grooming. These packages usually contain gifts such as blankets, toys, treats, Petco cards, and beautiful notes and letters from all around the world. When the mail lady showed up with no package, Josh would growl and bark. But if she had a package, he knew it was for him and he literally jumped up and down with excitement.

"Look what I have," the mail lady said as she entered. "I know I'm safe today."

Tina and Rita laughed as Josh bounced all around unable to control his enthusiasm.

"Thanks," Rita said as she collected the rest of the mail—bills.

Tina couldn't open the small box fast enough for Josh. Finally she pulled out a small squeak toy and handed it to him. He grabbed it and took off to his favorite corner and curled up with his new prize and began to suck on it, something he had begun doing of late.

Tina looked inside the box and saw an envelope. Pulling it out, she nodded at her mom.

"Oh, you have a note?" Rita asked. "Read it."

Tina pulled out the folded sheet of paper and read.

```
Dear Josh and Mom,
    Just a note to say "hel-
lo." I have been following your
page on FB since I was intro-
duced to you through another
page. I so appreciate the work
y'all are doing and the aware-
ness you bring for those born
with disabilities. You've saved
many lives and given our furry
friends a chance to live full
happy lives. Please stay in
touch. I hope to be of help in
some way.

    Love,
    Linda Burk
```

"That is so sweet," Tina said as she silently read the note again.

This had become common. She received so many uplifting messages through Josh's Facebook account. It was truly heartwarming.

After Tina left work that day, she took Josh over to the East Valley Veterinarian Clinic for a regular checkup. Josh loved to visit the vet because he was treated like a movie star there. Tina let him down as they entered the vet's office and Josh rushed to one person after another for attention. Pretty soon the entire staff was standing around him in a circle giving him treats and hugs. Josh was in Heaven.

There are also two cats there, Jojo and Jammer, and Josh has play dates with them. Josh loves all animals, even the cats, dog, birds, squirrels, and baby opossum now being fostered a Tina's.

Shortly after they got back to the examination room, Dr. Hohne, the owner of the clinic, came in. Dr. Hohne is a small guy with a soothing voice. He has been Josh's vet practically since Josh was born.

"Hey guys," Dr. Hohne said. "How are you today?"

Tina smiled and nodded and Josh wagged his tail.

The first thing the doctor did was check Josh's

heart. "He still has a strong heartbeat. That's a good sign. Now let's have a look inside your mouth."

The crack in the upper part of Josh's mouth was always a concern for the vet.

"How does it look?" Tina asked.

The vet looked up and shrugged. "It seems to be getting bigger as Josh gets bigger, but I still don't think it needs surgery. He seems to be getting along very well as it is."

Tina smiled at her little fellow. "What about surgery for the outside?"

The doctor shrugged. "Yes, it could help him look more normal. But it's not like with a human. I don't think Josh knows he's different."

Tina smiled. That was true. Besides, nothing could make him more beautiful to her. But she did have one concern. "What causes the really horrible breath?"

The doctor smiled. "Well, it could be food getting caught in the crack in his mouth." He took his light and looked into Josh's mouth again. "I don't see anything like that. It could just be juvenile Halitosis, which means we don't know what causes it. Try changing his food and make sure you keep him out of the cat box. We don't want him thinking those are snacks in there."

Tina giggled. "One more thing; he has starting sucking on his toys, like a puppy suckles. He carries around his toys like a mother does a puppy also, then nurses on the toy until he drifts off to sleep."

The doctor thought for a moment. "It might be just because Josh never had a doggie mom and he's making up for it. I wouldn't worry about it."

After they got home that evening, Tina signed on to Josh's FB to respond to numerous messages. She never let anyone contact Josh without a response, if nothing more than a quick "thank you." But one email got her attention.

"Oh my god!" Tina yelled. "Lenny, check this out."

Lenny walked up and peered over her shoulder. "What it is?"

"It's from a Dr. Patrick Mahaney. He says that he has heard about Josh and his story has inspired him to do a write-up on *Pet MD*." Tina turned to look at Lenny as a tear rolled down her cheek. "That's so neat."

"It really is," Lenny agreed.

Tina contacted Dr. Maheney and gave him the information he asked for. She was on Cloud Nine awaiting the article to run. Finally it did. Here are some excerpts.

The Internet's cuteness meter was recently taken by storm with the story of an adorable dog named Josh, who has a birth defect that limits his quality of life and the ability to properly eat and drink. Josh's condition is called a cleft palate and can be a life-limiting factor for a puppy's proper development.

Josh has overcome adversity and matured into an adolescent pooch having a unique lifestyle. In the petition to have Josh appear on the cover of Modern Dog magazine, we learn some interesting facts about this cute pup.

Age: 5 months
Nicknames: wolfie! bad boy! wild child!
Likes: cats, birds
Dislikes: He likes everything!
Favorite Foods: His puppy food
Favorite Pastimes: Playing at our grooming shop

What I love seeing is the outpouring of photos and kind

words on JOSH's Facebook page from other owners who have dogs that are affected by cleft palate, including Giget, a Chihuahua, and Treble, who also looks like a Chihuahua (or mix). There are also well wishes from pet lovers worldwide who are interested in seeing Josh continue to thrive.

What I find very interesting about Josh is that he has been able to thrive to the age of five months despite his medical condition. Having a cleft palate leaves an affected puppy, kitten, or other species especially prone to a variety of health concerns.

I hope that Josh continues to thrive in life despite his conformational abnormality.

Tina read the article aloud to Josh, who sat quietly looking up at her. "You're really something," she said looking down at her best buddy. "You know that?"

CHAPTER 5
A Star Is Born

Josh continued to thrive and make new friends. When he was ten months old, a fan named Donna emailed Tina and said, "*The Modern Dog Cover Contest* just started again. Go, go, go!"

Tina signed onto the computer, rushed to the website, and noticed it was the first day of the contest. She couldn't download his picture fast enough. The reason she wanted the cover so badly was to educate people about birth defects. Plus, when was the last time you saw a cleft palate on the cover of a magazine? Yeah… never. You always see a beautiful pure breed, right?

I would also love Josh's previous owner to see he is still alive. Oh, how I wish the previous owner could see Josh now, Tina thought as she worked on Josh's entry into the contest.

It wasn't to be mean; just to let them know they made a mistake. People need to understand that there is help out there and there is no need to kill animals over birth defects.

By this time Josh's FB page had fifty-three thousand fans. Tina posted the vote-link and added, "Let's try it again! We came in second place last time. LET'S DO IT!"

Everybody went crazy voting. Josh received two thousand votes in just a few hours. His fans were on a mission to win it. There were tons of comments.

"We are going to make sure you are going to win!!"

"There is no way you are getting second place this time, Josh!"

"Please remind us every day to vote!!!!!"

By now Josh had made tons of friends from other pet pages like *Munster*, an English bull dog born with Spina Bifita, *Rosie*, the cleft lip doggy, *Baby Zeke* with the cleftie smile, *Barney Rubble*, the cleft lip bulldog, *Stella*, the puppy mill survivor, and of course *Brogan, My Life as a Therapy Dog*, who was born with Addison's Disease. The list goes on.

Everybody was pulling for Josh and his critters. Josh's votes shot up and up and the race was on. This contest went for two months. It was the longest contest ever. Josh got so many votes. No one could come close to him. The other pups in the top ten were fighting for second place.

After the contest ended on Jan 7, 2015, Tina received an email. "Congratulations Tina & Josh. YOU HAVE WON!"

Of course Tina cried her eyes out.

"Are you going to be okay?" Lenny asked.

Tina wiped her eyes and smiled. "Yes. I think I am still emotional from the last contest. We tried so hard and it finally paid off. We got the cover."

They all went out to dinner to celebrate that night: Rita, Tina, Lenny; the whole Family.

Next came the big photo shoot in Hollywood, Ca. By now, Josh was just days away from turning one year old. *Modern Dog* sent an email and instructed them to take Josh to a photography studio on Wilcox Street in Hollywood. The photographer was a wonderful woman named Christina Gandolfo and she also had a wonderful assistant.

"What a beautiful fellow," Christina said as she scratched the top of Josh's head. "Let's get him ready."

They groomed Josh to perfection.

"It's time to shine, my little star," Tina told Josh. "You went from death row to cover dog."

Josh was ready but Tina was nervous.

"I don't know how he's going to act," she told

Lenny. "He is not going to sit still or behave. Remember, he is still young and he is a bit of a wild child. If Josh doesn't want to do something, he will let you know."

Lenny assured her Josh would do fine.

Josh was still a baby in Tina's eyes. She thought for sure he was going to give them a hard time.

They walked into the room where the photo shoot would take place. It was big and beautiful and so professional. Josh pranced in almost cocky. He was happy to be here. The girls knelt down to him and said hello and he was happy. Tina let him off the leach and he ran around and around the whole studio. They wanted him to be comfortable and got him some water, which he drank.

Now it was time to put him up onto the stand. It was a big table with a big backdrop. Up he went, and of course he jumped right down. They put him back up and back down he jumped again. So back up he went and Tina stood to the side of him and told him to stay while she stayed right there by him.

They snapped several photos like this. Next they came out with a big fan.

"Oh, my gosh," Tina said. "There is no way he is going to let you blow that in his face."

The photographer smiled. "Don't worry, Tina.

We are used to this."

On came the fan and Josh was almost in shock, but he stood still just looking at the fan as if he was mesmerized by it. He had one paw up and his head was tilted almost like trying to figure out what it was.

They got several shots and then let him get down. He grabbed his stuffed toy and took off running.

They showed Tina the shot they took with the wind and she was blown away. He looked so beautiful with his fluffy white hair blowing in the wind. He looked so amazing. Tina almost cried.

A lady walked in and introduced herself as Jennifer Nosek, Editor and Creative Director of *Modern Dog Magazine*. She was a pretty blond lady and very nice. She came all the way from Canada to meet with them and fell in love with Josh the minute she met him.

"I would love to get some outside shots," she said.

"We live across the street from a beautiful park," Tina offered.

Everyone agreed, so they all packed up and off they went. They arrived at Stonehurst Park and Josh was very happy. He knew exactly where he was because Lenny brings him here for walks all the time.

He was quite relaxed, so they put him in a tree on a big branch and he stood there like he was king of the mountain. They took his harness off so he could run. Lenny ran around and around and Josh was so excited. They took tons of action pictures.

"Tina," Christina said, "let get some of you and Josh."

That's what they did, and although Tina was nervous, she was excited as well. *Oh wow*, she thought, *I hope they put one of these pictures in the magazine. You never know.*

Of course they only took five pictures that way and then they were done.

"Would you guys like to swing by our grooming shop?" Tina asked afterward. "It's only two miles from here."

"Yes." Jennifer and Christina both agreed.

Once at Rita's Grooming, they all walked through the shop and the first critter they saw was a giant turtle weighing over a hundred pounds. They were in awe.

"Oh my gosh," Jennifer whispered.

Tina smiled. "That's Peek-a-boo, our rescued turtle. The owners could not afford to feed him so we took him. Everybody seems to think all they eat is lettuce but that's far from the truth. They eat the most pricy veggies like romaine, dandelion, and Timothy hay, and many different squashes, and they eat all day long."

"Kind of like me," Lenny joked.

Everyone laughed.

Josh ran over to greet his friend, Peek-a-boo.

"They also need special lighting when they live indoor," Tina continued. "Peek-a-boo is very happy where he is at today."

Christina took out her camera and started shooting the turtle.

Next they met Foxy the Pig. Josh acted like the host as if he was introducing everyone. Even at his young age, Josh had become the patriarch of the entire group, overseeing all the new arrivals and making them feel at home, and making sure to spend time with the current critters.

"Foxy was a handful for her previous owner," Tina explained, "and she was on her way back to the breeder, so Lenny and I got word of this and we went to pick her up. She gets into everything and screams when she doesn't get her way."

"So let's just say she always gets her way," Lenny added.

Tina nodded. "She is so cute and fat and smart. She can sit on command and sit up and spin, and she even has a bell she rings when we tell her to go ring the bell."

Tina gave her the command and Foxy obeyed. Christina and Jennifer couldn't believe their eyes. They took more pictures of Foxy.

One-by-one the dogs Tina and Josh fostered started coming out, so Tina gave the story for each.

"Hank is a fifteen-year-old brown terrier who was supposed to be a hospice case and was only going to last a week. That was a year and a half ago and he is still going strong.

"Sadie is a cocker mix white, who was rescued from the pound, but when they got her she turned on them. No one could touch her at first and she was so matted and skinny. Her fur was like a shell; she was in bad shape and biting at everyone." It was one of the hardest jobs Tina ever had, grooming Sadie, and it took four months to get her to trust again.

"We have two cats that live at the shop named Fuzzylumpkin and Cherry, also rescues. They both came in motherless and I hand-raised them too."

Christina took pictures of everyone.

They walked into the back and met Tina's mom, Rita, and Topogigio, the rescued opossum. "He also came in as a motherless critter and was hand raised," Tina said.

The ladies loved him and fed him some grapes and took pictures of him as well.

"He lives in a strawberry house and he snuggles like a cat," Tina said. "He has no idea he is a opossum. He walks around with Hank, Sadie, Peekaboo, and Foxy, and everybody gets along."

Then they met Kevin and Tiny, the rescued squirrels and took pictures of them.

"Normally the squirrels I rescue can be released, but Kevin and Tiny are special-needs critters, so they live here at the shop and love it."

Tina then introduced them to two gophers. "I just rescued these guys."

The ladies smiled again. They seemed to be amazed at the range of critters that Tina and Josh rescue, even the ones that most people consider pests.

"We believe everybody deserves a chance, right Josh?" Tina patted Josh on the head and he wagged his large tail to show he agreed. "We will never turn an animal away of any kind."

The time had come for the ladies to leave, so Josh walked them to the front door. Everyone hugged and said their goodbyes.

Five days later, Tina received an email from Jennifer. It read, "We love you and Josh so much we are putting you both on the cover."

I'm Not Defective: The Story of Josh

Tina cried and cried. "You are truly special," she said as she looked down at Josh and patted him on the head. "Look at all the incredible things you've accomplished and you're not even a year old."

Josh paying a visit to the residents of the Windsor Court Assisted Living in Plam Springs

AFTERWORD

Josh continues to make all the rescued critters feel at home and to inspire people and pets all around the world. He turned one year old on January 20th, 2015. You can follow Josh and all the rescued animals on Facebook under the name J*osh and his critters*.

Modern Dog Magazine with Josh and Tina on the cover hits newsstands in March 2015.

Tina recently took in another puppy that a homeless man dropped off, as well as six birds, one of which is a Birmingham Roller pigeon. Lenny is happy because he is a Birmingham Roller enthusiast.

QSDC Magazine, a publication that promotes Birmingham Rollers, contacted Tina recently and will be presenting her a Lifetime Achievement Award for her work with birds and other animals. Mike Tyson is slated to present the award in March 2015.

The End

Modern Dog Spring 2015 hits newsstands March 15th

www.ingramcontent.com/pod-product-compliance
Lightning Source LLC
Chambersburg PA
CBHW041928040426
42444CB00018B/3464